RESURRECTION
WITNESSES

By
Dwayne Norman

Empyrion Publishing
Winter Garden FL

Resurrection Witnesses
ISBN: 978-0692225011
Copyright 2014 by Dwayne Norman

Empyrion Publishing
Winter Garden FL
info@EmpyrionPublishing.com

Unless otherwise indicated, all Scripture quotations are taken
from the New King James Version of the Bible.

TABLE OF CONTENTS

1

The Importance of Jesus' Resurrection

The greatest witness to the resurrection of Jesus is another resurrected man or woman! I don't personally know anyone who's been physically raised from the dead, but I believe many have been. I do know that every Christian has been raised from the dead spiritually. So, spiritually speaking, we are all resurrected men and women. Think of how powerful our witness to the world will be, when we really learn how to live like resurrected men and women; when we learn to live out of the resurrection realm! It's the same supernatural realm Jesus lived out of and walked in during His earthly ministry. We're called and anointed in Him to do the same things (John 14:12-14), to walk in and minister from the same supernatural realm! We need to better understand how important Jesus' resurrection was, because it greatly affects our lives today.

I Peter 3:21,22

"There is also an antitype which now saves us-baptism (not the removal of the filth of the flesh, but the answer of a good conscience toward God), <u>through the resurrection of Jesus Christ,</u>

Who has gone into heaven and is at the right hand of God, angels and authorities and powers having been made subject to Him."

The Bible tells us that Jesus has gone into Heaven and is sitting at God's right hand, but the end of verse 21 says it was <u>through His resurrection.</u> Please remember that. The reason He is seated at the Father's right hand, and everything is subject to Him, is because of His resurrection. Now, let's tie this in with Hebrews 4:14.

"Seeing then that we have a great High Priest who has <u>passed</u> <u>through the heavens</u>, Jesus the Son of God, let us hold fast our confession."

The reason Jesus has gone into Heaven (referred to as the third Heaven. The location of God's throne and the departed saints), is because He passed through the heavens (or the second heavens). Again, the reason He passed through the heavens, was because of His resurrection. So, the resurrection is very important! Just how important is it? Well, according to the Apostle Paul, in I Corinthians 15:17, he said:

"And if Christ is not risen your faith is futile; you are still in your sins!"

Notice, he didn't say if Christ did not die you're still in your sins. Jesus' death was very, very important, but he said our faith would be worthless and useless if Jesus did not rise from the dead. When I teach on the Mystery of Christ (see our book, "The Mystery", workbook and DVD's), we take time to look at seven areas of our redemption. Before Jesus went to Calvary, He suffered at the hands of man. He sweated Blood in the Garden of Gethsemane. By His 39 stripes we were healed. Then, He was crucified, He died, was buried, made alive (spiritually), conquered the devil and all of Hell, was resurrected and seated at the Father's right hand.

Every one of these areas is very important. There could be no resurrection without a death. It's hard to raise someone from the dead that's not dead. Jesus' resurrection is proof that He died, and our changed lives is proof that He arose. Even other religions believe Jesus was a good man, a good teacher, a prophet and that He died, but they only see Him dying as just another martyr. They don't believe He arose from the dead, and is now the Lord of lords and the King of kings. The bones of all the other religious leaders are still buried in their graves, but not Jesus! He's alive and well and has the keys of Hell and of death! The devil doesn't want us preaching any of the

Gospel, but he especially hates it when we talk about Jesus' resurrection. So, let's talk about it more! That's why I'm writing this book! Look what Paul said when he was brought up before the chief priests and all their council.

Acts 23:6

"But when Paul perceived that one part were Sadducees and the other Pharisees, he cried out in the council, "Men and brethren, I am a Pharisee, the son of a Pharisee; concerning the hope and <u>resurrection of the dead I am being judged!"</u>

I heard one minister say that everywhere Paul went he always had revival or riots, one of the two. He was probably one of the greatest soul winners who ever lived. He's the one who told us, in II Corinthians 5:18,19, that God has given the Church the ministry of reconciliation (soul winning). You know the devil despised him and wanted to stop his ministry. Paul told us why he was being judged everywhere he went. He said it was because of preaching about the resurrection of the dead. He was telling people they could be resurrected spiritually into newness of life, and one day be raised into their immortal bodies. This is all possible because Jesus arose from the dead in our place. He identified Himself with us at Calvary. He fully represented us when He arose. Therefore, His resurrection is our resurrection!!

If you notice, Paul didn't say he was being judged for preaching on love (as important as that is), and we need to walk in love all the time. He didn't say he was being judged for feeding the poor, did he? We need to feed the poor, the bible teaches that, but he wasn't being judged for that. These are all good things that show we're disciples of the Lord, but Paul didn't say he was being judged for these things. Now look at Acts 24:17-21.

"Now after many years I came to bring alms and offerings to my nation,

In the midst of which some Jews from Asia found me purified in the temple, neither with a mob nor with tumult.

They ought to have been here before you to object if they had anything against me.

Or else let those who are here themselves say if they found any wrongdoing in me while I stood before the council,

Unless it is for this one statement which I cried out, standing among them, 'Concerning the resurrection of the dead I am being judged by you this day.'"

This was when Paul gave his defense before Felix the governor. The Apostle Paul preached a lot of good things. He wrote almost two thirds of the New Testament. He taught all the council of God, yet he said he was being judged for <u>one</u> statement. I find that very interesting. He could have said he was being judged for 3, 7 or 10 statements, but out of all the many things he preached, he just named this one: **The resurrection of the dead**. Wow! The devil must really hate that subject, so let's talk about it a lot!

Acts 4:1,2,33
"Now as they spoke to the people, the priests, the captain of the temple, and the Sadducees came upon them,

Being greatly disturbed that they taught the people and preached in Jesus <u>the resurrection from the dead</u>.

And with great power the apostles gave witness to <u>the resurrection of the Lord Jesus</u>. And great grace was upon them all."

First of all, the religious leaders were greatly disturbed at what Peter and John were preaching. It was actually the devil in these leaders who was so disturbed. He didn't like them preaching on the resurrection. Again, it didn't say they were greatly disturbed because they preached on walking in love, feeding the poor, reading your Bible everyday and going to church.

Granted, the devil is very opposed to all those things, but what greatly disturbed him, was the preaching of the resurrection. All those other good things one can do, and still not be a Christian. Godly works are wonderful, and the devil doesn't like them, but they won't give a person eternal life. Great humanitarian programs are very good, and we need them in every town and city, but they're not the source of eternal life. Only the Lord Jesus can give eternal life. The devil would rather you talk about feeding the poor, than Jesus' death and resurrection. The Bible doesn't say if you feed the poor you will be saved. It says if you confess Jesus as Lord, and believe in your heart that God **raised** Him from the dead, you will be saved (Romans 10:9).

Lots of churches have many great outreaches that bless their community, and we need that. Many of these churches though, spend more time preaching about all their good programs than preaching about the death and resurrection of Christ. The programs should be used as a witnessing tool to lead the lost to Jesus. The devil doesn't mind it so much if we feed people why they remain in his kingdom, but I guarantee that when you start explaining to people what Jesus' resurrection means to them, you'll begin encountering more resistance. You'll start getting judged like Paul was, but that's ok, you're on the right track. You're not only helping people with their physical necessities, but you're bringing resurrection life to them and changing their spiritual destinies. Keep clothing and feeding the poor, but also tell them of the death and resurrection of Christ and what it means to them.

Verse 31 in Acts 4 says, with great power they gave witness to the resurrection. We will see a lot more results and greater demonstrations of God's power when we proclaim Jesus' death and resurrection. The Lord put His power in that message (I Corinthians 1:18; Romans 1:16). This was why Paul had riots (the devil in people being disturbed), and revivals everywhere he went. I see why Paul was being judged. I also see why he had miracles, signs and wonders everywhere he went. The power of God was constantly flowing in his meetings, and it wasn't because of the great programs he offered. It was because of the message he preached! Let me give you another example, in Acts 17:2,3,18,32.

"Then Paul, <u>as his custom was</u>, went in to them, and for three Sabbaths reasoned with them from the Scriptures,

Explaining and demonstrating that the Christ had to suffer and <u>rise</u> <u>again from the dead</u>, and saying, "This Jesus whom I preach to you is the Christ."

Then certain Epicurean and Stoic philosophers encountered him. And some said, "What does this babbler want to say?" Others said, "He seems to be a proclaimer of foreign gods," because he preached to them Jesus and <u>the resurrection</u>."

And when they heard of the <u>resurrection of the</u>

dead, some mocked, while others said, "We will hear you again on this matter.""

In the first verse we read, it says as his custom was. Preaching Jesus and His resurrection was Paul's custom, meaning it was something he did all the time. This wasn't just a message he thought would be nice for this particular group of people. We need to make this our custom as well, in all our churches. That doesn't mean all you can say, every time you get up to preach, is Jesus died, was buried and arose from the dead. That's not what we're saying. Remember, Paul taught all the council of God. He taught on other subjects from the Word. So, we just need to make sure all of our teaching goes through Calvary. For example, if I'm teaching on marriage, I would explain that the main reason we can have a successful marriage, is because of what the Father did for us through Jesus' death and resurrection. The reason we can love each other like Jesus loves the church, is because we've been resurrected with Christ and we now have His love working in us.

Let me remind you of something else that shows how important the resurrection of Christ was. Genesis 1:1 says that God created the heavens and the earth. If you notice, the word earth is singular, and heavens is plural; meaning there's more than one heaven. The Bible tells us there are three heavens. In II Corinthians 12:2,4, Paul said he was caught up to the third Heaven or Paradise. Well, logic dictates, if there's a third Heaven, there must be a first and second. The third Heaven is the location of God's throne room. The first heaven is the atmosphere above the earth, where we live. The second heaven is everything between the first and third, or space. The Bible calls it the heavenlies (see our book, Going up To the High Place).

The Scriptures talk about how angels and wicked spirits operate in the second heaven. Now, these are not things we see down here with our natural eyes. We know from the Word that a lot of what takes place on the earth, in governments and people's lives, is a direct result of spiritual battles fought in the heavenly realms. The perfect example of this was in Daniel, chapter 10. Remember, Daniel lived before Calvary took place, so the devil had not yet been defeated, and man had not been redeemed.

An angel of the Lord came to Daniel 3 weeks after he had prayed. It took him 21 days to get to Daniel. He was late because he had to fight his way through the prince and kings of Persia. He wasn't talking about human beings on the earth. He was talking about evil spirits (principalities) in the second heaven. There was some kind of spiritual barrier there, and the angel couldn't get through it. So, God sent Michael, one of His chief princes to help him. Think about how strong one of God's angels is. The Bible says that the angel of the Lord went out, and killed in the camp of the Assyrians one hundred eighty five thousand (II Kings 19:35). Just one angel did that, but now in Daniel's situation, this particular angel couldn't pass through the second heavens to get to him without Michael's help. I said all that to emphasize how powerful Jesus' resurrection was. When He arose from the dead, He passed right through the second heaven, and there wasn't a thing the devil could do to stop Him! He passed right through that spiritual barrier. He didn't get stuck there for 3 weeks. A resurrected man passed through the heavens and sat down at God's right hand. Only a resurrected man could do that, <u>and that's what we are in Christ</u>! When Jesus passed through the heavens and sat down, we passed through and sat down in Him! You can better understand why Paul was judged for preaching in Jesus the resurrection. The devil doesn't want people to know this, because he loses control over them. Now, go back with me to Hebrews 4: 14-16.

"Seeing then that we have a great High Priest who has passed through the heavens, Jesus the Son of God, <u>let us hold fast our confession</u>.

For we do not have a High Priest who cannot sympathize with our weaknesses, but was in all points tempted as we are, yet without sin.

<u>Let us therefore come boldly to the throne of grace</u> that we may obtain mercy and find grace to

help in time of need."

In verse 14, he's telling us how Jesus passed through the heavens then he tells us to hold fast to <u>our</u> confession. Why would he tell us about Jesus' great victory then tell <u>us</u> to hold fast to <u>our</u> confession? He would only do that if there's a connection between us and the resurrection of Christ. If someone told me that a wealthy business man just became a billionaire through the success of his company, I would probably be glad for him, but I would have no reason to be glad for me. It's wonderful that he's a billionaire, but how does that help me pay my house payment? But, if you told me that this business man just became a billionaire, and put me in his will, now I'm not only rejoicing for him, but I'm rejoicing for me. There's a connection now between him and me. Whenever you meditate the Word, you want to look for the connections between you and Jesus, because everything He suffered and finished at Calvary was for our benefit. It wasn't just so we could rejoice that he became a billionaire, so to speak. This connection is confirmed in I Peter 1:3.

"Blessed be the God and Father of our Lord Jesus Christ, who according to His abundant mercy <u>has begotten us</u> again to a living hope <u>through the resurrection</u> of Jesus Christ from the dead."

We are begotten or born of God, through Jesus' resurrection. Now, look back at verse 16, in Hebrews chapter 4. We're told to come boldly to the throne of grace. Think about this with me. We're told to <u>come there</u>. I've heard Christians say when they pray, they like to imagine themselves traveling to God's throne room, going through the gates of Heaven and sitting down at the Father's right hand. That sounds real nice, and it makes for a good song, but it's really not quite correct. He's not saying that some of you are about 2 miles out from the throne room, but if you keep fasting and praying enough, and pressing in there, you'll make it in. It's time the Church moves up to a higher level of thinking, then we will operate in a higher level of believing. Ephesians 2:4-6 tells us that <u>we</u> have been made alive, resurrected and seated together in Christ at the Father's right hand. The Bible says <u>we</u> are already there. We're not trying to get there one of these days. God <u>has already </u>made us to sit at His right hand! So, why would He tell us to come there, when we know from His Word, we're already there?

Since we're already there in Christ, then there must be another point He's trying to get across to us. He must be talking about boldly expecting to experience all the benefits of our place at the Father's right hand. We need to see ourselves as already there in the spirit. We're not hoping to get there.

I believe when God says to come boldly to His

throne of grace, He means we need to get a reality of our connection with Christ and start walking in it. He's encouraging us to expect everything He's done in our lives to come to pass! Expect to experience all the power and blessings of our new position in Christ! Don't be satisfied with just knowing what your position is. Expect to live it out on this earth! Here is what you need to picture in your heart and mind.

Picture Almighty God sitting in His seat in the throne room. Now, see God turn His head slightly to the right, (and if your name is Jim or whatever), hear Him say, "Hi Jim. I'm glad you're here." In my mind, I see Him say, "Hi Dwayne. I'm glad you're here." Because I am, in the spirit, in Christ, I'm not trying to get there! I'm not trying to come there! I'm already there! I live there every day! Even though I'm on this earth in my physical body, in Christ I'm seated (past tense) at my Father's right hand! Praise the Lord! It's all because of the resurrection!

Remember, by His resurrection, He passed through and went into Heaven. Do you see why the devil hates the resurrection? Do you see why the Apostle Paul was persecuted and attacked so much? The devil did everything he could, even sent a thorn (a demon spirit) to try to hinder him from preaching this message, but the devil lost! Paul finished his race and fulfilled what God called him to do, and so will we! It's time we start acting and living like resurrected men and women! Let's be the kind of witnesses to the resurrection of Christ that He created us (in Him) to be!!

I've been ministering in churches for over 30 years, training believers in Supernatural Evangelism and who they are in Christ. Even though I teach Soul Winning seminars, that's not what motivated me to go witnessing. It was in 1977, while attending Christ for The Nations Bible School, in Dallas, Texas, I began to learn how to witness. I like to tell people that my motivation to witness did not come from attending a great Soul Winning seminar. It came as I began learning who Jesus is. Who He is in me, and who I am in Him. What the Bible refers to as the Mystery of Christ. Paul was commissioned to teach this to the Church in Ephesians, chapter 3.

I had been reading the books of Kenneth Hagin Senior and E. W. Kenyon and getting very excited about the Lord! I heard Brother Copeland's testimony of shutting himself in the garage and listening to all of Kenneth Hagin's tapes. After hearing that, I decided to do the same thing (not go to the garage though), but with Kenneth Copeland's tapes. His office was in Ft. Worth, which was about 45 minutes from the Bible school. I had one of his catalogs, and even back then, he had a lot of tape series on many different subjects. I spent most of the money I made on the Word. I figured it would be a good investment. About every 2 weeks I would go to Brother Copeland's office and buy $100.00 to $140.00 worth of tapes, and listen to every one of them. I continued doing this until I listened to everything in his catalog.

I got so full of the Word, I didn't need anyone to encourage me to go witnessing. Even though I was new to this, I was so stirred inside from learning who I am in Christ that I had to tell someone. So, I just started walking down the highway from the men's dorm and began talking to different people about the Lord. You can go to a dozen Soul Winning seminars, but if they don't teach you who you are in Christ, you probably won't stay motivated very long. In the past, a lot of Soul Winning teaching has been very boring. Someone comes in and gives a lot of questions you may be asked, and 2 answers for each question. They spent much of their time teaching Believers how to intellectually out debate the lost, almost making it into a contest to see who is the most persuasive, many times resulting in arguments. Yes, it's very important to learn God's Word, and to have answers for questions you'll be asked, but it's also time to see God's Kingdom demonstrated in power. That's where having a revelation of what it means to be identified with Jesus in His death and resurrection comes in. As Christians, we're stirred up and set on fire to operate in our ministries by getting a revelation and greater understanding of our connection with Jesus in His death and resurrection.

2

Imitating Christ

What greatly builds up my faith and encourages me to fulfill the great commission in my life, is learning that a resurrected <u>man</u> defeated the devil and his entire kingdom, and a resurrected <u>man</u> is sitting at God's right hand in Heaven! I Timothy 2:5 says:

"For there is one God and one Mediator between God and men, the Man Christ Jesus."

Beck translation says: **"There is one God, and One who brings God and men together, the Man Christ Jesus."**

Jordan translation says: **"For God is one, and there is one connecting link between God and man - the Man Christ Jesus."**

I Corinthians 15:21 says:
"For since by <u>man</u> came death, by <u>Man</u> also

came the resurrection of the dead."

It's extremely important that you understand that all the healings, miracles, signs and wonders Jesus did, He did as a <u>Man</u> anointed with the Holy Spirit and power. He didn't do anything as God. People want to believe He did, but he didn't. He said if we believe in Him, we will do the same works He did, and greater works in His Name (John 14:12-14). If He did anything as God, then we could not fulfill these verses. Now, Jesus was all God and all man in one individual, but He laid aside His glory as God to operate as an anointed man. Even though He was God, He didn't work any miracles as God. He did that for our benefit, to demonstrate what we can do now, anointed with the same power. He knew before He came here that we're not God and never will be. He knew the only way we could carry on His ministry, is by showing us it could be done without being God. He proved to us what a man or woman of God can do, totally yielded to the Holy Spirit! So, knowing what Jesus did as a man, lets me know that I don't have to be God to do what He's called me do. I can rest in being a man in Christ. Wow! If that doesn't build your faith, I'm not sure what will. Christians have said, "Well I'm just a man. I'm not Jesus." Implying that the works He did were a result of Him being God. They don't see themselves ministering to people as Jesus did, because in the back of their minds they still think He had something special they don't have, or He was the only one God would allow to act like Him.

Because of this, some will say, "You just think you're God." My answer to them is, "No!! It's just the opposite of that. I don't have to be God or think I'm God to act like Him, and do His works. I get to do that as a man!" It's all through the anointing of the Holy Spirit, and we will look at that later. Our Father God even instructed us to imitate Him. Ephesians 5:1 says:

"Therefore be imitators of God as dear children."

Only <u>resurrected</u> men and women can imitate God. But what does that mean to imitate God? Again, some think you have to be God to act and talk like Him, but you don't. You can be a man (or woman) and do that, as long as you've been <u>raised</u> (spiritually) from the dead. The King James Bible says, **"Be ye therefore followers of God…"** In the Kenneth Wuest Word studies, he said in the Greek, the word "be" means to become, and the word "followers" means imitators; it's where we get our word "mimic". The dictionary defines imitate as an attempt or endeavor to copy or resemble. I believe this word imitate has a higher meaning than the way we use it in the world. Follow me in this. If I want to imitate John Wayne, then I am going to try to talk and act like he did. It's all about me trying to be like he was. So I would have to watch his movies over and over again, until I developed his mannerisms and started walking like he walked. This is the way many in the Church interpret Ephesians 5:1. They put forth all their human effort (flesh) to try to act like God, or at least be a good reflection. It's not about how talented we are in mimicking God. That's the way the world imitates people. Isaiah 60:1-5 says:

"Arise, <u>shine</u>; for your light has come! And the glory of the Lord is risen upon you.

For behold, the darkness shall cover the earth, and deep darkness the people; but the Lord will arise over you and His glory will be seen upon you.

The Gentiles shall <u>come to your light</u>, and kings to the brightness of your rising.

Lift up your eyes all around, and see: they all gather together, they come to you; your sons shall come from afar, and your daughters shall be nursed at your side.

Then you shall see and become radiant, and your heart shall swell with joy; because the abundance of the sea shall be turned to you. The wealth of the Gentiles shall come to you."

Here's a saying I've heard for years, "As Christians, we are a reflection of God's light." Then they'll use the example of the Sun and moon. They'll describe the Church as the moon, which reflects the light of the Sun (Son). The moon has no light, it's just reflecting the Sun's light. Isaiah didn't say to arise and reflect. He said to arise and shine. We don't reflect Jesus' light, we <u>are</u> light in Him (Ephesians 5:8)! If you take a burning coal out of a fire full of coals, that one individual coal is on fire and lit up. It's not reflecting anything. It's on fire! We are on fire, and we are light in the Light (Jesus)!

The Living Bible says:

"Arise, my people! Let your light shine for all nations to see! For the glory of the Lord is streaming from you. Darkness as black as night shall cover all the peoples of the earth, but the glory of the Lord will shine from you.

All nations will come to your light; mighty kings will come to see the glory of the Lord upon you."

A number of years ago, when I lived in Lexington, Kentucky, I had the privilege of leading my neighbor to the Lord. I was thrilled he got saved, but it was kind of an unusual experience. I was sitting in my living room on Sunday afternoon, around 4pm, when I saw him walk up to my front door. I had only met him once, and that was a very brief introduction. Other than that one moment, we never spoke to each other again. When I answered the door, I was kind of light hearted, trying to be friendly, but quickly realized he didn't feel the same way. As soon as I said hello, he responded by saying, "I was going to commit suicide, but I thought I would come see you first." Wow! I didn't expect to hear that. I was stunned. I invited him in and we began to talk. I said, "Since you're being very serious with me, let me be very serious with you. I know I could give you a bunch of nice platitudes, and tell you everything is going to be alright, but let me get right to the point."

So, I asked him if he had ever been born again. Without hesitating, he said no. I said, "Even when you were much younger, you never prayed and asked Jesus to come into your heart and be the Lord of your life?" He responded with a solid no. I then told him that the most important thing he could do right now, is to become a child of God, and that the Lord really loves him and wants to help him. I explained how God wanted to bring him into His Kingdom, so He could bless him. I asked him if he believed that Jesus died and arose from the dead. He said he did. So, I led him in a prayer to receive Jesus into his life, and he got saved! You don't have to get emotional, but it seemed that the Lord really touched and ministered to him that afternoon. We talked a while longer, and I shared some more things with him on how to live for God. Before he left, I asked him why he came over to my house, since we didn't know each other. He said he was in his backyard thinking about committing suicide, when a voice spoke to him, and said, "Before you do that, go and talk to the man next door." Praise the Lord! I believe that was God who spoke to him. After he said that, I was reminded of Isaiah 60, where it said the Gentiles will come to your light. Now I know we're called to go into all of the world and preach the Gospel to every person, but it's nice when they come to you. The glory of God will draw them to us. God can speak to you to go to them, but He can also speak to them to come to you. Isn't that great?

Now listen closely. Imitating God is more than God giving us power to imitate Him. <u>He gives us Himself</u>! Imitating the Lord is not about us trying to talk and act like Him. It's simply about us yielding to His Spirit within us, and letting Him speak through our lips, and lay hands on people through our hands. It's not about you and me trying to do anything. That's why we can rest in the peace of God every day, because we know it's not about us. We're just earthen vessels that the excellence of God's glory flows through. Our job is to learn to yield, and let Him have His way in us; that's imitating God. In the King James Bible, I Corinthians 1:30 says:

"But of him are ye in Christ Jesus, who of God is made unto us wisdom, and righteousness, and sanctification, and redemption."

We don't try to imitate God's wisdom. The Lord

Jesus is made unto us wisdom. Just allow His wisdom to flow through you. We don't have to try to imitate all that Jesus is made unto us. We just surrender to His nature within us, and allow Him (His nature) to be expressed through us. You can't imitate fruit. An orange tree can't imitate an apple tree. The nature of the orange tree is to produce oranges.

I Peter 1:15,16 says:

"But as He who called you is holy, you also be holy in all your conduct,

Because it is written, "Be holy, for I am holy.""

God told the Church to be holy, for or <u>because He is holy</u>. If you ask many Christians why God is holy, they'll say because He's God. If you think about it, that can't possibly be true, or God has commanded us to do something that's impossible for us to do. If you have to be God to be holy, then we will never be holy, because we will never be God. So, there must be another reason God is holy. He's holy because that's His nature. Guess what? You have His nature (II Peter 1:3,4). You and I will never be God, but we do have His Divine nature operating in our reborn spirits. Again, to imitate God is not something <u>we try</u> to do. The kind of imitating the Bible is referring to, is through **<u>impartation</u>**! We've received an impartation! You may ask, "An impartation of what?" It's not what. It's who. The Lord has imparted His

28

Spirit within us. If I want to imitate the president, the most I can do, is to talk and act like him. The president can't jump inside me, and then live his life through me; but Jesus can. Can you see that this is a much higher form of imitation than is demonstrated in the world? It's Galatians 2:20. I taught this in my book "Defending the Faith", but it's needful for me to share some of it again. In the King James Bible it says:

"I am crucified with Christ; nevertheless I live; yet not I, but <u>Christ</u> <u>liveth in me</u>; and the life which I now live in the flesh I live by the faith of the Son of God, who loved me, and gave himself for me."

The Apostle Paul taught that the old me (the old man), or my sinful nature was crucified with Christ. He's dead and gone. The "I" who lives now is a brand new "I", or man. But look closely at what I underlined in that verse. Paul defines the new "I", as Christ liveth in me. So, God's definition of the new "I", is Christ liveth in me, that's who I is. I know it's not correct grammar, but you won't forget it. Whenever I think of "I", or the word "I", I think of the definition. "I" is Christ liveth in me; that's who "I" is! Instead of saying, "I can preach the Gospel." I could substitute the definition and say, "Christ liveth in me can preach the Gospel." I don't ever say, "I can't witness to people" because it would be like saying, "Christ liveth in me can't witness to people." Do you see how understanding this will give you a greater boldness, knowing you are not by yourself anymore? Christ liveth in me can do anything! The Distilled Bible is my favorite translation of this verse.

"I consider myself as having died and now enjoying a second existence, which is simply Jesus using my body."

Now that is a resurrection man! That is imitating God! In Acts 14, Paul and Barnabas imitated the Lord so well, the people said, **"The gods have come down to us in the likeness of men."**

And in Acts 28, Paul was bit by a snake, shook it off and felt no harm. Verse 6 says, **"However, they were expecting that he would swell up or suddenly fall down dead. But after they had looked for a long time and saw no harm come to him, they changed their minds and said that he was a god."**

3

The Anointed Man

All the works Jesus did was as an anointed Man. He depended totally on the anointing of the Holy Spirit. Acts 10:38 says:

"How God anointed Jesus of Nazareth with the Holy Spirit and with power, who went about doing good and healing all who were oppressed by the devil, for God was with Him."

Because we are resurrected men and women, there's an anointing that accompanies that resurrection. There were great benefits that came with your resurrection in Christ. The Lord Jesus made it very clear that He could do nothing by Himself. He said the Father did the works through Him (John 14:9,10). He was a vessel for God's anointing to flow through. The same is true for us today. I'm so glad I don't have to be God for His anointing to flow through me. I can be a man, exactly who God created me to be. The word "anoint" means to smear or rub on. If I was at the beach, my wife could anoint me with suntan lotion, it's the same meaning. When you and I received Jesus, and were born again, we didn't lose our humanity. When we got saved, we were resurrected from spiritual death to spiritual life. After being born again, we could be filled with the Spirit, according to Acts 1:8, and be anointed or covered all over with the Spirit and power of God. The Lord's plan was to use men and women to carry out His work on the earth. God wanted to show through Jesus in the four Gospels, and through all Christians today, that He can work supernatural miracles through us, without making us God. That's how powerful and great His anointing is, for without it, we're just mere men. Remember, Jesus was God when He was 15 years old, as well as 30 years old, but He never worked any miracles until He was <u>anointed</u> (when He was baptized by John and the Spirit of God came upon Him). Since He didn't minister as God, He had to be anointed. John chapter two tells us His first miracle was turning water into wine, but He did that after He was anointed.

The Lord Jesus said, **"For I have come down from heaven, not to do My own will, but the will of Him who sent Me."** (John 6:38) The Father's will was to show that a human being, with God's anointing, could do the works of God. I got to thinking one day about how difficult it must have been for Jesus to resist operating as God. Before He came here, think of everything He saw and did as God for eternity past. He was all powerful, all knowing, and present everywhere. There were and are no other gods beside Him. Everything was created through Him. His Name is Almighty God! But, God told Him He had a plan for man, and even though He was God, in this plan He could not operate as God. He told Him He would do all the miracles God could do, but He would have to do them as a man. And since men can't heal or work miracles by themselves, He would give Him an anointing that would enable Him to do these things. So, I assumed it must have been a very strong temptation for Jesus to resist operating as God; but as I thought about it more, I began to realize I was wrong. I don't believe it was a temptation for Jesus at all, because He knew how powerful the anointing of the Spirit was. He had such great confidence in that enablement, and what the Father by the anointing could do through Him, He never thought of operating as God!

I hope you see where I'm going here. You and I have the same anointing (I John 2:20,27; II Corinthians 1:21)! Think about how great the Spirit and power of God is within us! Think about that for a minute! We have God's anointing within us and upon us! Inside and outside! Because we are in Christ, we can also say that the Spirit of God is upon us and He has anointed us to minister to the people (Luke 4:18)!

Jesus did all the works of God without doing them as God. He did them all by the anointing, and we get to operate in the same anointing now!! We definitely need a greater reality of what we have in Christ! Let's start depending on His anointing to flow through us to do the works of God; that is why He anointed us! If that anointing, which came freely by God's grace (Hebrews 2:9), was more than enough for Jesus, then it's definitely more enough for you and me.

The anointing of God's Spirit and power enabled the Lord to pay the penalty of sin for all humanity, to obtain eternal redemption for us, to conquer all of Hell and sit down at God's right hand, as the Lord of lords! That's why I don't think about trying to be God. I don't need to. I have His anointing through His grace! His anointing is more than enough for me. Jesus was God on this earth, but He never healed or worked miracles because He was God. The anointing upon Him was all sufficient. Think about this with me. To be anointed with the same anointing that Jesus operated in is tremendous! We are anointed with the same anointing that enabled Jesus to do the works of God, without operating as God. That's awesome! That helps me to relax, knowing that I don't have to perform. It's not about me. It's about yielding to the Spirit of God and allowing His anointing to flow through me. That's how Jesus ministered to the people. I didn't have that anointing before I was resurrected with Christ, or before I was born-again.

Now, that I am in Christ, I can be a witness to His resurrection!

So, before we continue, let me remind you of a few verses you can make note of, that describe the Deity of Christ, and His humanity.

"The Deity of Christ"

Romans 9:5,

"...Christ came, who is over all, the eternally blessed God. Amen."

Titus 2:13,

"...Our great God and Savior Jesus Christ."

I John 5:20,

"And we know that the Son of God has come and has given us an understanding, that we may know Him who is true; and we are in Him who is true, in His son Jesus Christ. This is the true God and eternal life."

Revelation 1:8,

"I am the Alpha and the Omega, the Beginning and the End," says the Lord, "who is and who was and who is to come, the Almighty.""

"The Humanity of Christ"

Luke 2:52, He grew intellectually and physically.

"And Jesus increased in wisdom and stature, and in favor with God and men."

Matthew 4:2, He desired food.

"And when He had fasted forty days and forty nights, afterward He was hungry."

John 4:6, He became tired.

"...Jesus therefore, being wearied from his journey..."

Matthew 8:24, He needed sleep.

"...the boat was covered with the waves. But He was asleep."

John 19:33, He died.

"But when they came to Jesus and saw that He was already dead..."

The Lord Jesus was and is all God and all man in one person, but His ministry on the earth was only as a man anointed with the Holy Spirit and power. Look with me at Mark 2:5-7, something the scribes said when Jesus told the paralytic his sins were forgiven.

"When Jesus saw their faith, He said to the

paralytic, "Son, your sins are forgiven you."

And some of the scribes were sitting there and reasoning in their hearts,

"Why does this Man speak blasphemies like this? Who can forgive sins but God alone?"

Why did they think He was blaspheming? They thought you have to be God to forgive. So, they assumed He must think He's God, since He forgave the man. They totally missed it. Jesus wasn't trying to prove to them He was God, and He didn't forgive the man because He was God. They missed it on both counts. They missed it like many in the Church have missed it today. The only conclusion they could come to was, since only God can do these miraculous works, then He must think He's God. They didn't have a spiritual clue that an anointed <u>man</u> could do the works of God. That thought never occurred to them, and what's also sad to say, is that thought has never occurred to many Christians today.

Not once did Jesus try to convince anyone that He was God, and we're not here to convince anyone that we're God. Our witness is to the resurrection of Christ, and that <u>He</u> is Almighty God. That's why we're anointed. We are spiritual soldiers with a mission to carry out, and we don't have to do it in our own strength. He's fully equipped us with all we need. Just be a yielded vessel, and let the Holy Spirit have His way. The Lord Jesus did that from the very beginning of His ministry, from His baptism in Mark 3:16,17.

"When He had been baptized, Jesus came up immediately from the water; and behold, the heavens were opened to Him, and He saw the Spirit of God descending like a dove and alighting upon Him.

And suddenly a voice came from heaven, saying, "This is My beloved Son, in whom I am well pleased.""

I got to thinking about Jesus' baptism, and realized it was very symbolic for the anointing coming upon resurrected men and women. Baptism in water is an outward symbol of an inward grace. When you go under the water, it shows that you (your old man or nature) died and were buried with Christ. When you come out of the water, it shows you arose to newness of life. That's why sprinkling someone on the head with water is not Biblical baptism. Sprinkling doesn't show a person's identification with Jesus in His death and resurrection. John didn't sprinkle Jesus, and Philip didn't sprinkle the eunuch in Acts 8. But notice what happened. After Jesus came up from the water, or you could say the grave, the heavens were opened. After He came up from the water, symbolically showing the resurrection, the heavens were opened, and the Spirit of God came on Him like a dove, reminding us again, that by His resurrection He passed right through the heavens (that spiritual barrier). When He came up from the water, or was resurrected, the anointing came on Him to start His ministry. The devil hates the resurrection! He can't stop resurrected men and women. Think of it like this. When we came up from the water, the heavens were opened, and the anointing of God came on us to start and to fulfill our ministry in Him.

When we were resurrected with Christ, the heavens were opened unto us. Let's learn to live and minister out of the resurrection realm, which is learning to minister in His anointing. Since we are men and women who depend on God's anointing, let's learn everything we can about it. I heard one minister say that <u>what you host and are conscious of, is what will be released from you</u>. What a powerful truth! What you host is what you honor, what you pay attention to, and what you spend time learning about. The more conscious I become of God's anointing in my life, the more time I spend learning about that anointing, and how to flow in it; the more it will be released from me.

The Apostle Peter hosted God's presence and power so well, when the sick got within shadow distance of him, they were healed (Acts 5:15,16). We should expect that to happen in our lives! Now, what you host can work in the negative sense, and the positive. If a person spends their time hosting things that are ungodly and unclean, that's what will be released from him. Psalm 109:17-20, in the Amplified Bible says:

"Yes, he loved cursing, and it came [back] upon him; he delighted not in blessing, and it was far from him.

He clothed himself also with cursing as with his garment, and it seeped into his inward [life] like water, and like oil into his bones.

Let it be to him as the raiment with which he covers himself and as the girdle with which he is girded continually."

The Lord said this man loved or hosted cursing so much, he gave such great attention to cursing, it became like a garment he wore. The Psalmist said it even seeped or soaked into his inward life like water, and went into his physical bones. In other words, he hosted cursing so much it became a part of him. Think about people who smoke continuously. It seems to soak into them. They stink all the time. They get around you and your clothes start stinking. What a rude habit, but that's what the Word said would happen. They try to take mints, and do things to eliminate the smell, but it usually doesn't work. They're wearing that cigarette smell like a garment everywhere they go. It becomes part of them. Well, we don't want those things to become part of us. We don't want those things soaking into our bones. The same is true for unforgiveness, bitterness, jealousy and strife. If you give your attention to those things and start hosting them, they will also seep into your bones, and you may not realize it, but you'll begin wearing those things like a garment. If you don't notice it, other people will. It's a principle that works positively or negatively (Proverbs 4:20-22).

Just think what will happen, if we host God's presence. If we make a habit of spending time studying who we are in Christ, and how to operate in God's anointing. That's what we'll be conscious of all the time, and that's what we'll wear as a garment. If we will spend time everyday worshipping the Lord and soaking in His glory, His power, love and holiness, even His fire will soak into our very bones; until we become radiant with His glory!

The Prophet Jeremiah said, **"...But His word was in my heart like a burning fire shut up in by bones..."** And remember, when a dead man was let down on the dead bones of the Prophet Elisha, he came back to life. Elisha hosted the anointing so much during his life, that after he was dead, there was enough power left in his bones to resurrect a man! (II Kings 13:20,21)

Resurrection Witnesses

4

What Direction Does the Anointing Flow?

Look with me at a number of verses in Ezekiel 47, starting with verses 1&2.

"Then he brought me back to the door of the temple; and there was water, flowing from under the threshold of the temple toward the east, for the front of the temple faced east; the water was flowing from under the right side of the temple, south of the altar.

He brought me out by way of the north gate, and led me around on the outside to the outer gateway that faces east; and there was water, <u>running out </u>on the right side."

In the Bible, water is used symbolically to represent the Word of God (Ephesians 5:26), and the Holy Spirit (John 7:38,39), which includes His anointing and presence. For Ezekiel, the temple was the same as the local church is to us. It's very important that every Christian is a faithful member of a New Testament church. That's a church that teaches the uncompromised Word of God and flows in the gifts and ministries of the Holy Spirit. I believe that every Christian needs to be under the teaching of a pastor, and should attend church on a regular basis (Hebrews 10:25; Ephesians 4:11,12; Acts 4:23; 5:42; 13:1). We need to bring all our tithes into the local church, and support other ministries with our offerings. The local church is where we are to be taught and trained to do the work of the ministry.

What stood out to me one day when I was studying this, is that water was <u>running out </u>of the temple; not running into it. I think over the years, many of us have had an incorrect understanding of the direction the anointing flows. Let me explain. I've heard many ministers say, "Bring the lost to church (the temple), so they can be saved. Bring the sick to church, so they can be healed." And yes, that's true. If we don't get the lost saved before we come to church, then bring them to church. If we don't get the sick healed before we come to church, then bring them to church to get healed. But the mindset that has been developed in a lot of Believers is that all the supernatural miracles done by God for people must be done in the church. So, in essence, we've taught Christians that most of the time salvations, healings and miracles will be done for people, if we can get them to our local church for the pastor to minister to them. I know the pastor will be glad to minister to them, but that's not his main job. His ministry is to teach and train the saints to do the work of the ministry. And where's the <u>main place </u>we are to do the work of the ministry? In our church? No, in the world, where most of the population is. The local church is where we are trained to go out. Three times the Lord Jesus told Peter to feed (train) His sheep. He didn't tell him to do the work of the ministry for the sheep. Sheep produce sheep. I know, spiritually, the shepherd is also a sheep, but Jesus set the shepherd (pastor) in the church to be a feeder.

Since water is symbolic for the anointing of God, then the anointing was flowing out of the church (temple). It wasn't flowing into it. Yes, it was coming from the church, but flowing out into the world. This is very important! The anointing flows out, into the world; not from the world into the church. Now, let's look at verses 3-5 in this chapter.

"And when the man went out to the east with the line in his hand, he measured one thousand cubits, and he brought me through the waters; the water came up to my ankles.

Again he measured one thousand and brought me through the waters; the water came up to my knees. Again he measured one thousand and brought me through; the water came up to my

waist.

And again he measured one thousand, and it was a river that I could not cross; for the water was too deep, water in which one must swim, a river that could not be crossed."

What excites me is the water got deeper the further away Ezekiel got from the church (building). The water getting deeper represents the anointing increasing! It represents the Spirit and power of God being manifested stronger! If you notice, it wasn't reversed. The water or anointing wasn't getting deeper, the closer he got to the temple. Christians will say, "I know I can lay hands on the sick at work, but I want to get them to church, where the anointing is stronger." This kind of thinking can be a hindrance to the expansion of God's Kingdom. Christians won't be as excited about taking time to minister God's power to people in the world, if they don't believe His anointing will be there. They won't expect the Lord to do as much, if the teaching they're hearing implies that there will be a greater anointing if you can get them to church.

In verse 1, it said the water was flowing from under the threshold of the temple. Threshold means a piece of wood or stone beneath a door, entrance or doorway place, or point of beginning, outset. Some think they don't need to come together in the local church, but their thinking is totally unscriptural. Also, verse 12 says the water flows from the <u>sanctuary</u>. It's the threshold, the source where the water comes from. When we (Christians) come together, the Lord will manifest His corporate anointing and presence, to soak and saturate us even more, while the Spirit of God trains us. Then we (as the spiritual church) can take that anointing out into the darkness, so they can see the light. As we go, God will cause His anointing on us to increase the further out we get, or the more the people need it. While we're out there ministering to the lost, we will also invite them to come back to church with us, so they can be taught and trained to do the same things. Our mind set should be, "I'm going to take this anointing into the market place where the lost and sick are." Ezekiel 47:6-9 says:

"He said to me, "Son of man, have you seen this?" Then he brought me and returned me to the bank of the river.

When I returned, there, along the bank of the river, were very many trees on one side and the other.

Then he said to me: "This water flows toward the eastern region, goes down into the valley, and enters the sea. <u>When it reaches the sea, its waters are healed</u>.

And it shall be that every living thing that moves, wherever the rivers go, will live. There will be a very great multitude of fish, because these

**waters go there; for they will be healed, and
<u>everything will live wherever the river goes</u>."**

In the Bible, a sea can be a real sea, or it can be
symbolic for peoples. Here it represents multitudes of
people. These waters (this anointing of the Holy
Spirit and power) are to go into the valleys where the
people are. They're to flow into the lives of people
who are in the valley of death, sickness, poverty and
depression. These people need to be set free. They
need to meet the risen Christ Jesus. These waters
don't flow to the people by themselves. The Lord
takes His power and love to people through us. Isaiah
10:27 tells us that the anointing breaks the yoke. You
are God's vessel to take them this anointing!
Resurrected men and women have been equipped to
do this! You're qualified in Christ! Don't forget
God's promise as you go. He said everything will live
wherever the river goes! Wherever the anointing
goes! So let's expect that to happen everywhere we
go, because that's everywhere the river goes!

Back in verse 5, he said the water became too
deep for him to cross. Up until then, he could stand
up in his own efforts. Theologians tell us that 1000
cubits is about one-fourth of a mile, so going out 1000
cubits, 4 times, would be about 2 miles. It wasn't
until he got far enough out, that the water or the
anointing took him over, and began to carry him.
That's what we want to experience. In the first 3000

cubits, human effort was still involved, and had control over the river, but when he got to the place where he had no more control, and had to totally rely on the river or anointing, then all the waters of people were healed. John 3:34 says:

"For He whom God has sent speaks the words of God, for God does not give the Spirit by measure."

God gave the Lord Jesus, His Spirit or anointing without measure. Jesus was the entire body of Christ on the earth at that time. He operated in all the ministry gifts. He did it all. As individual Believers, we don't have His Spirit without measure to function in all the ministries, and to operate as all of the body, but we do have His Spirit and anointing without measure to do what He's called us to do. If He's called you to be a knee in His body, then He's given you everything you need to do that. God said He already anointed us in Christ (II Corinthians 1:21)!

If we will learn the lesson God taught Ezekiel, we will start experiencing the anointing we already have. One way to host that anointing and become more conscious of it, is by going into the world of hurting, suffering people and ministering to them in Jesus' Name. The more we yield ourselves to the Holy Spirit and allow Him to have His way, the deeper the river will become in our lives. That's what the anointing is for, to set the captives free! Let's yield so much to the Spirit of God, that we give Him full control, so it's not about our human effort any more. That's what it means to walk in the spirit and not in the flesh. That's when God's river gets so deep in our lives, we can't cross it any more. Then we let the river, the anointing of the Holy Spirit take us where God wants us to go.

5

The Church on Fire

We should be so on fire for the Lord that other Believers catch on fire by just being around us! That's what fire does! It sets things on fire!

Acts 28:1-10 says:

"Now when they had escaped, they then found out that the island was called Malta.

And the natives showed us unusual kindness; for they kindled a fire and made us all welcome, because of the rain that was falling and because of the cold.

But when Paul had gathered a bundle of sticks and laid them on the fire, a viper came out because of the heat, and fastened on his hand.

So when the natives saw the creature hanging from his hand, they said to one another, "No doubt this man is a murderer, whom, though he has escaped the sea, yet justice does not allow to live."

But he shook off the creature into the fire and

suffered no harm.

However, they were expecting that he would swell up or suddenly fall down dead. But after they had looked for a long time and saw no harm come to him, they changed their minds and said that he was a god.

In that region there was an estate of the leading citizen of the island, whose name was Publius, who received us and entertained us courteously for three days.

And it happened that the father of Publius lay sick of a fever and dysentery. Paul went in to him and prayed, and he laid his hands on him and healed him.

So when this was done, the rest of those on the island who had diseases also came and were healed.

They also honored us in many ways; and when we departed, they provided such things as were necessary."

We've mentioned before about symbolism in the Bible. Many times natural truths are designed to reveal spiritual truths. In these Scriptures we looked at, we know that the Apostle Paul was headed to Rome, but got delayed in a ship wreck. He and the crew landed on an island called Malta. The natives there were very kind and had a <u>fire</u> already going, because it was <u>rainy</u> and <u>cold.</u> It also sounds like a lot of sick people were on the island before Paul arrived. Remember, rain or water is symbolic for the Word, the Holy Spirit and His power (the Anointing). Even though they had a fire going, and it was raining; it was still <u>cold</u>. Cold representing the fact that nothing spiritually significant was happening in the people's lives before Paul arrived. But let's look at what happened. The fire was already going, but Paul wasn't satisfied with it. It wasn't hot enough for him. Now, he may not have realized the spiritual truth that God would one day reveal to us from his encounter. He just wanted it to be warmer, but the Holy Spirit likes to take stories like this and teach us spiritual lessons from them.

Listen closely. Many in the Church are like these natives. They're very satisfied with the fire they have, even though they're seeing no salvations, healings or miracles. What I mean by that is, they're satisfied with where they are spiritually with the Lord, even though nothing is happening in their lives. They are spiritually comfortable. They are not hungry. They are experiencing what firemen call a <u>controlled burn.</u> It's a fire they are monitoring closely, so it won't grow, expand or get out of hand. Sometimes, firemen will start another fire to put out a bigger one. They call it a controlled burn. They guard and watch it closely so it doesn't get out of control. A lot of Christians are like that. They want God in their lives, but they want to control Him. They're what the Bible describes as having a form of religion, but denying the power of it (II Timothy 3:5). They want to yield enough to the Lord to look religious, but not to let the Holy Spirit have His way in their lives. These types of Christians will never experience revival in their lives. Even though it may be raining where they are (because the presence of God is everywhere), their lives will always be spiritually cold; unless they follow Paul's example.

What did Paul do when he wasn't satisfied with the temperature of his present condition? He put more wood on the fire! He wasn't trying to have a controlled burn. He wanted some heat, because the fire they had wasn't producing enough. The fire in a lot of churches is not producing enough heat. They need to turn it up. The way they turn it up is by the individual believers turning up God's fire in their lives. We need to start putting enough spiritual wood on our fires until all the cold or spiritual lethargy is gone! It's not mainly up to our pastors, it's up to each one of us. As Christians, we are ministers of fire!

Psalm 104:4 & Hebrews 1:7 says:

"Who makes His angels spirits, His ministers a flame of fire."

When the Lord speaks of His ministers here, I believe He's not just referring to his angels as ministers, but also to Christians. I know His angels can appear in fire, but Hebrews also says God is a consuming fire. Ephesians 5:8 says we are light in Him (Who is light). Since He's a consuming fire, and we're in Him, then we must be ministers of fire. In the Tabernacles of Moses, fire came down from God and consumed the sacrifice on the altar. It was God who originally started the fire when they set up the Tabernacle. They weren't using a box of matches to start the fire. It was supernaturally started. Then the priest took the fire into the Tabernacle to light the candlestick. It was up to the priest to keep the fire going after God started it (Leviticus 9:23,24; II Chronicles 7:1-3; Acts 2:3). On the Day of Pentecost, God set the Church on fire. Tongues of fire sat upon each of them. God started the fire, but it's up to you and me to keep it going. It's up to us to put wood on the fire. I heard a minister say that someone had asked John Wesley many years ago, why he had such large crowds to preach to. His answer was, "I set myself on fire and the people come out to watch me burn." Obviously, he meant spiritually, not physically. We need to start thinking that way. I want to stay on fire for God all the time! Don't you?

Luke 5:17 says:

"Now it happened on a certain day, as He was teaching, that there were Pharisees and teachers of the law sitting by, who had come out of every town of Galilee, Judea, and Jerusalem. <u>And the power</u>

of the Lord was present to heal them.

This is the story of the paralyzed man being healed, after his friends let him down through the roof of the house where Jesus was teaching. According to this verse the crowd was so thick from the amount of people there, the only way they could get the man to Jesus was through the roof. It also says the power of the Lord was present to heal them, meaning everyone there; but we only have record of this one man being healed. Remember, we must operate in faith to activate God's power to produce results. When the paralyzed man and those carrying him saw the heavy crowd, they could have said forget it, turned around and gone home. They could have stayed satisfied with the man's present condition, or remained content with the fire they had, but it wouldn't have produced the results the man needed.

Many of us have not experienced the blessings of the Lord and been used in ministry the way God desires, because our fire is not hot enough. In the King James Bible, Psalm 104:4 says He makes His ministers a <u>flaming</u> fire. The Hebrew word for flaming is "Lahat", it means to lick, to blaze, and to set on fire. This definition describes the nature of fire. I especially like the last part of the definition "to set on fire". **The nature of fire is to set on fire.** In other words, it can't be still or quiet. It can't remain to itself, and leave everything around it alone. Its very nature is to set everything it touches on fire. Praise the Lord! That definitely describes God's Church! Our very nature in Christ is to set everyone on fire with God's love, power and presence! Everywhere we go, the works of the devil should be burned up, and the works of God manifested!

Think about lighting a match. If you drop it in some dry grass, the fire won't stay where the match lands, it will begin to spread, won't it? It can't help it. That's its nature. As Believers, we don't need to try to set others on fire for God. We don't need to try to witness and talk to people about the Lord. When you're on fire for the Lord, it will come out of you everywhere you go. You can hardly wait to share the Gospel and minister to people! Why? Because that's your nature! If you don't feel that way, then that's a sign or evidence that your fire is not hot enough. Let me remind you of what the Lord told the priest in Leviticus 6:12,13.

"And the fire on the altar shall be kept burning on it; it shall not be put out. And the priest shall burn wood on it every morning, and lay the burnt offering in order on it; and he shall burn on it the fat of the peace offerings.

A fire shall always be burning on the altar; it shall never go out."

The New Testament counterpart to that is found in

Paul's letter to Timothy.

II Timothy 1:6,7 says:

"Therefore I remind you to stir up the gift of God which is in you through the laying on of my hands.

For God has not given us a spirit of fear, but of power and of love and of a sound mind."

Paul was actually telling Timothy how to (spiritually) put more wood on his fire. He said to stir up the gift of God within you. W. E. Vine's Greek dictionary says, the word "stir" or "stir up" denotes to kindle afresh, to keep in full flame, and is used metaphorically in verse 6, where the "gift of God" is regarded as a fire capable of dying out through neglect.

The New Living Translation says, **"This is why I remind you to fan into flames the spiritual gift of God."**

The Easy To Read Bible says, **"Now I want you to use that gift and let it grow more and more, like a small flame grows into a fire."**

I think it's possible that some ministers and pastors don't know the difference between a controlled burn and Divine order. They may be getting them mixed up. They think they are keeping Divine order by not allowing anyone to step out in faith and flow in the gifts of the Spirit. They don't want to deal with people getting in the flesh, or doing things not inspired by God. Well, I don't know any minister who looks forward to dealing with people who yield to their flesh instead of their spirit. No one likes to clean up other people's messes. Many of those Believers though, will turn out to be powerful ministers of the Lord, if we will be patient and take time to disciple them. But, that's the way life is, and that's the way church life is. All of us are learning better everyday how to walk in the spirit and not in the flesh. The important thing is that we are willing to receive correction and make changes in our lives. If you're going to have increase, growth and prosperity, you have to take risk, and you have to know you're going to clean up some messes. I would rather have growth and increase, and clean up some messes, than have no messes and no growth. Proverbs 14:4 says, **"Where no oxen are, the trough is clean; But much increase comes by the strength of an ox."** I heard one minister say there is no such thing as a poopless cow. We want to have a lot of cows, so to speak, but we don't want to clean up their messes. If you don't want any messes, you won't have any cows.

That's why Paul wrote the letter to the Corinthians; especially I Corinthians chapter 14. He was writing to encourage and instruct the church in God's order, and clean up some messes. Verse 1 & 39 says:

"Pursue love, and desire spiritual gifts, but especially that you may prophesy."
"Therefore, brethren, desire earnestly to prophesy, and do not forbid to speak with tongues."

Paul was writing to a group of Believers in Corinth who knew how to operate in the gifts of the Spirit. He said they came short in no gift (Chapter 1, verse 7), and when they came together, each of them had a psalm, a teaching, a tongue, a revelation, and an interpretation (Chapter 14, verse 26). Those people weren't afraid to step out and prophesy in their services; so Paul wasn't writing to convince them to operate in the gifts. He was instructing them how to operate in God's Divine order. After reading Chapter 14, it sounds to me like everyone in the congregation was trying to flow in the gifts and speak messages in tongues at the same time, and they needed some practical training. I think if most ministers today had written to this church, it would have been to tell them to calm down and not step out so much. What I find very interesting is, the Spirit of God had Paul do the opposite of that. Before he talked to them about order in the church, he encouraged them further about flowing in the gifts. Look again at Chapter 14, verses 1 & 39. Instead of watering down their fire, it's seems that God wanted to pour gas on it, and make it even hotter; despite the fact they needed training in how a congregation should flow in the Holy Spirit. He said you need to desire spiritual gifts, but especially to prophesy.

Let me give you an example of how this sounds. Let's say there was a church that shouted all the time, through praise and worship, and even through the preaching; and the Lord led me to write them a letter of instructions regarding their services. If I followed Paul's example, I would first say, "You all need to greatly desire to shout in your services, desire earnestly to shout!" Then, after saying that, I would go on to explain to them there is a time to shout and a time to be quiet. There is an order for everything. You see, before God began explaining about Divine order, He first encouraged them to operate in the gifts. What's that mean? It means the Lord will never take wood off your fire. He will never pour water on your fire as His way of teaching you Divine order. God will always stir us up to step out in faith, but to remember to use wisdom and be led by the Spirit.

Remember, when Paul told Timothy to stir up the gift (fan the flame) within him, He also said that God has not given us a spirit of fear or timidity, but of power and love and a sound mind (II Timothy 1:7). Many times we use this verse to claim freedom from a fear of snakes, flying, diseases, storms, etc...and that's ok; but Paul was telling Timothy that God had not given him a spirit fear or timidity in stirring up the gift in him. He was saying, "Don't be afraid to fan that flame! Don't be afraid to put more wood on your fire! Don't be afraid to step out and prophesy! You have everything you need! My power, love and a sound mind!" Let's look one more time at a few verses we read in Acts 28: 3-5.

"But when Paul had gathered a bundle of sticks and laid them on the fire, <u>a viper came out because of the heat</u>, and fastened on his hand.

So when the natives saw the creature hanging from his hand, they said to one another, "No doubt this man is a murderer, whom, though he has escaped the sea, yet justice does not allow to live."

But <u>he shook off the creature into the fire </u>and suffered no harm."

I want you to notice why the viper or snake came out. It was because of the heat. The natives had a fire going before Paul arrived, but there was no evidence of snakes at that time. Some Christians say that they have a fire going all the time, and the devil, for the most part, leaves them alone. All I can say is the viper didn't come out until Paul put more wood on the fire. The devil hates all of God's people, but he especially wants to stop those that are a threat to his kingdom. I've said this before, but I want to say it again. There are 2 main reasons the devil attacks

Christians: 1. Because they're not serving God. They're backslidden. 2. Because they are serving God. Either way the attacks will come. The devil's goal is to eliminate all Christians, but he can't do it, because we have all power over him in Jesus' Name! You can experience tests and trials because you're not serving God, and opening up a door in your life for the devil to get in. If you're in that condition, repent, ask God to forgive you, and close that door (I John 1:9).

You can also experience tests and trials because the devil is trying his best to discourage you, and stop you from preaching the Gospel. Just resist him in Jesus' Name and he will flee from you (James 4:7). If you're serving the Lord with all your heart, and experiencing conflict in your life, that's a good sign. Conflict in that case is a sign you're progressing, and doing what God has called you to do, so rejoice. The Lord Jesus experienced tests and trials. In Luke 22:28, He said, **"But you are those who have continued with Me in My trials."** Think about the Apostle Paul's testimony in II Corinthians 11. Other than the Lord, he was probably attacked more than any Christian living at that time. For both of these men, it wasn't because of their lack of faith that trials came, but because of their strong faith. No matter how much they were attacked, no matter how many vipers came out because of the heat, the devil still lost, and they won! Jesus' Name was glorified and the

Kingdom of God was demonstrated!

Jesus and Paul knew what to do with the snakes. Just shake them off into the fire. That's one of the benefits of having a hotter fire. It will consume all the snakes! Jeremiah 23:29 says:

""Is not My word like a <u>fire</u>?" says the Lord, "And like a <u>hammer</u> that breaks the rock in pieces?""

One of the ways to "shake off the viper" is by speaking God's Word. Speaking what you believe will come to pass. It releases God's power and His fire to destroy what the devil's doing, and set the captives free! If the devil attacks you with sickness believe and declare, "By Jesus' stripes I'm healed!" Expect the fire of God's Word to go into that sickness and disease, and burn it up! Totally consume It! Remember, you're a minister of fire! Release that fire everywhere you go! It will destroy all of the devil's works, and bless God's people! Revival will break forth and the Word of God will be published throughout the land!!

6

The Militant Church

Listen to what the Lord Jesus said in Matthew 11:12.

"And from the days of John the Baptist until now the kingdom of heaven suffers violence, and <u>the violent take it by force</u>."

Luke 16:16 says:

"The law and the prophets were until John. Since that time the kingdom of God has been preached, and <u>everyone is pressing into it</u>."

The Church is made up of resurrection men and women, men and women who have been raised from the dead with Christ. Men and women who spoiled, rendered powerless and conquered the devil, and all evil principalities and powers (Colossians 2:15)! We are the spiritual army of the Lord (See our book, God's Elijah Army)! In the natural realm, armies are very militant. When the military from 2 countries go to war, they don't go out and play checkers. They engage in physical warfare, they have weapons to fight with. Their goal is to destroy the enemy and take the land, or to set the people free from a tyrant. That kind of military is very violent. If you read the book of Joshua, you'll see that Israel, under Joshua's command, was very militant. God told them to go take the land, and they did. They were very violent, but understand that their enemies would have destroyed them had they not been militant themselves.

Today, the Church is to be the same way, just not physically violent. Our enemy is the devil, demons and the curse. We love people, and we hate the devil attacking them; so we're to be very militant when it comes to the works of darkness! While we operate in the compassion of Jesus for the hurting, we resist the devil and don't give him any place! In Military terms you could say, protect the civilians and destroy the enemy. Dake's Annotated Reference Bible gives us the Greek definition of the word violent.

"To use force: To force one's way into a thing. The idea here is that before John the kingdom could only be viewed in the light of prophecy, but now it was preached, men pressing into it with ardor resembling violence or desperation. They appeared as if they would seize it by force.

It expresses the earnestness that men must have in getting rid of sin, all satanic powers, the world,

and in standing true when relatives oppose them.
(Matthew 10:34-39)

To me, it sounds like being so on fire for God, so committed to do His will that we won't let anybody or anything stop us! Like our Lord, we walk in love towards everyone, but we <u>don't</u> compromise God's Word! Jesus is always our first love, and we will never allow anything to sever that relationship (Revelation 2:4)! In the notes of the Spirit Filled Life Bible for Matthew 11:12, it says:

"The idea in this verse is that the kingdom of heaven, which Jesus set up as a powerful movement or reign among men (suffers violence), requires of them an equally strong and radical reaction. The violent then who take it by force are people of keen enthusiasm and commitment who are willing to respond to and propagate with radical abandonment the message and dynamic of God's reign.

The upheaval caused by the kingdom of God is not caused by political provocation or armed advance. It is the result of God's order shaking relationships, households, cities, and nations by the entry of the Holy Spirit's power working in people."

Resurrection men and women are soldiers of the

Lord.

"You therefore must endure hardship as a <u>good soldier</u> of Jesus Christ.

No one engaged in <u>warfare</u> entangles himself with the affairs of this life, that he may please him who enlisted him as <u>a soldier</u>." (II Timothy 2:3,4)

Soldiers engaging in warfare sounds militant to me. He's not talking about physical warfare, but spiritual warfare.

"For though we walk in the flesh (a physical body), we do not <u>war</u> according to the flesh.

For the weapons of <u>our warfare</u> are not carnal (natural, physical) but mighty in God for pulling down strongholds."

Again, in the Old Testament, Israel engaged in physical warfare. Satan wanted to wipe them off the face of the earth, in hope of stopping the Messiah from being born. Before Calvary, the people were not born again, and the Kingdom of God was not abiding in the hearts of men. But we can still learn spiritual lessons from their natural lessons (I Corinthians 10:11). We can gain great insight for engaging in spiritual warfare, by studying the successes of their physical warfare.

Judges 3:1,2 says:

"Now these are the nations which the Lord left, that He might test Israel by them, that is, all who had not known any of the wars in Canaan

(this was only so that the generations of the children of Israel might be taught to know war, at least those who had not formerly known it).

God told the children of Israel that He wanted them to be taught to know war. What did He mean by that? In our day, you'll hear parents who were in the military say, "I was in the military and fought for my country so my children will not have to go to war when they get older." God said there were Israelites who had not known the wars of Canaan, but instead of saying He was glad they didn't experience those wars, it seemed He said the very opposite. He actually wanted to make sure that everyone was taught to know war. Obviously, what He had in mind was not how we think about war today. When we say we don't want our children to know war, we're saying we don't want them to experience the death, pain and sufferings of war. When the Lord said for His people to be taught to know war, He wasn't saying, He wanted them to know what it's like to get stabbed, beat up or lose a loved one.

First of all, He didn't say I want them to be in a war. He said I want them to be <u>taught</u> to know it. He wanted them to know who their enemy was, his tactics and strategies, and how to defeat him if he attacks them. Back then, the Lord was talking about Israel's natural enemies, but now, for the Church, He's talking about our spiritual enemies. We learn how the devil operates by studying the Bible. The Spirit of God will teach us how to thwart his plans and destroy his strategies. Jesus already conquered the devil for us, and now we have been sent to demonstrate his defeat as God uses us in establishing the Kingdom of God in the hearts of men! Here is something else I want you to see. As soldiers of the Lord, we're also watchmen of the Lord. Yet another reason we should know how to engage successfully in spiritual warfare.

"Now it came to pass at the end of seven days that the word of the Lord came to me, saying,

"Son of man, I have made you a watchman for the house of Israel; therefore hear a word from My mouth, and give them warning from Me:

When I say to the wicked, 'You shall surely die,' and you give him no warning, nor speak to warn the wicked from his wicked way, to save his life, that same wicked man shall die in his iniquity; but his blood I will require at your hand.

Yet, if you warn the wicked, and he does not turn from his wickedness, nor from his wicked way, he shall die in his iniquity; but you have delivered your soul."" (Ezekiel 3:16-19)

Let me give you the Greek definition of a watchman from the Spirit Filled Life Bible.

"To look out, peer into the distance, spy, keep watch, to scope something out, especially in order to see approaching danger, and to warn those who are endangered."

As the militant Church, we have a responsibility to go into all the world and preach the Gospel to every person (Mark 16:15-18). Please don't misunderstand what God told Ezekiel. As an individual Believer, my job isn't to preach the Gospel to every person on the earth. I couldn't do that by myself. My responsibility to the Lord, is to preach His Word to everyone He tells me to speak to. That's one of the functions of a watchman. If the Lord speaks to me and tells me to warn someone of the dangers of Hell, and I don't do it, then He will hold me responsible. That's strong isn't it? But, that's what we just read. He doesn't hold me responsible for someone He told you to witness to. That's why I don't wait to see what other Christians are going to do, before I obey God.

Also, as the militant Church, made up of resurrection men and women, we're to be watchmen over our families, over our churches, over our governments and our nations. We have a responsibility to the people. Jesus told us to <u>watch</u> and pray. Through prayer and the gifts of the Spirit, we need to believe God to show us ahead of time what the devil's plans are, so we can stop them with the anointing. We need to be so established in the Word and in hearing God's voice, that we can distinguish wolves from sheep, false doctrine from true doctrine (See our book, Defending The Faith). We need to know who our enemy is, his tactics and strategies. We need to be taught (from God's Word) to know war. But know this, the best offense we can have, and the best defense will come by getting to know Jesus, who He is in us and who we are in Him. This is another area of being militant. In Philippians 3:13,14, Paul said:

"Brethren, I do not count myself to have apprehended; but one thing I do, forgetting those things which are behind and reaching forward to those things which are ahead.

I press toward the goal for the prize of the upward call of God in Christ Jesus."

When you make up your mind that you're going to forget the things of the past, that you have been forgiven and cleansed, and the old man (the old nature) is dead and gone, the devil will do everything he can to remind you of your past. Remember the Apostle Paul's testimony (Acts 26:9-11). He had a terrible past before he got saved. He delivered Christians up to be imprisoned and killed. You know the devil tried to remind Paul of his past. Paul learned from God to be very violent or aggressive (in the spirit) with his faith in resisting the devil. We have to do the same thing! Don't patty-cake around with the devil. Let him know he has no place in your life anymore, you're a brand new man (or woman) in Christ, and he has no dominion over you (James 4:7)! Like Paul did, press into the things of the Lord with everything within you! Determine you are going to be all God wants you to be, and successfully do all He wants you to do in Jesus' Name! The mind of a watchman, just like a soldier, is not concerned about himself. His face is set like flint on following the orders of his commander until he gets his job done. That should be the mindset of the militant Church! It's really not about you, and it's not about me. It's about what can God do through you and me for His Kingdom and glory on this earth!

Acts 1:8 says:

"But you shall receive power when the Holy Spirit has come upon you; and you shall be witnesses to Me in Jerusalem, and in all Judea and Samaria, and to the end of the earth."

The Greek word for power is "dunamis" and it means miraculous power, ability, <u>violence</u>, and worker of miracles. Years ago, when I first read that definition, I was surprised to see the word "violence" in there. What does violence have to do with working miracles? When we operate in God's power to heal the sick, lead sinners to the Lord and work miracles, we're being very violent in the spirit against our enemy, against the one holding the people in bondage. Where the people are concerned, we're using God's power in love and compassion to set the captives free; but in setting them free, we're wreaking havoc on the devil's kingdom. We are destroying it, and casting it out of people's lives in Jesus' Name!

Also in the Greek, the word "witness" is where we get our English word "martyr". It means to give up one's life. But don't mistake it for just physical death. Yes, many have physically died over the years for the Lord, and there will be more who will give their lives that way. But listen. If Jesus was only referring to physical martyrdom in this verse, then there wouldn't be any Church on the earth to carry out God's plan. Another way to be a martyr for the Lord is to give up your life, in life. In essence, that's what a true soldier does. While he's a soldier, he gives up his life to the one he's following and taking orders from. He also gives up his life for the people. He will do whatever needs to be done to help and protect them.

Let me remind you of one more thing. As the militant Church we have special keys. The Lord Jesus said, **"I am He who lives, and was dead, and behold, I am alive forevermore. Amen. And I have the keys of Hades and of Death."** I'm so glad that

Jesus has the keys, but what excites me even more, is that He gave them to us (His body)!

Matthew 16:19 says:

"And I will give you the keys of the kingdom of heaven, and whatever you bind on earth will be bound in heaven, and whatever you loose on earth will be loosed in heaven."

The Lord Jesus has given His body, or His army the power of binding and loosing. I know the term "binding and loosing" is not that familiar to people today. To put it in more modern language, we would say forbidding and allowing. What you bind is what you forbid. What you loose is what you allow or permit. Even though verse 19 says what you bind <u>will be</u> bound, and what you loose <u>will be</u> loosed; in the Greek language we're told it reads a little different than that. Listen to a couple of other translations.

Williams Translation says:

"I will give you the keys of the kingdom of heaven, and whatever you forbid on earth must be what is <u>already</u> forbidden in heaven, and whatever you permit on earth must be what is <u>already</u> permitted in heaven."

Amplified Bible says:

"I will give you the keys of the kingdom of

heaven; and whatever you bind (declare to be improper and unlawful) on earth must be what is <u>already</u> bound in heaven; and whatever you loose (declare lawful) on earth must be what is <u>already</u> loosed in heaven."

Here is what the Lord was telling us. Whatever we bind or forbid from operating down here (on earth), is what is already forbidden from operating in Heaven. The way to know what to forbid here, is to think about what's forbidden in Heaven. There is no sickness or disease in Heaven, so we have the power in Jesus' Name to forbid sickness and disease from operating in our bodies down here! In the Bible, keys are symbolic for authority and power. Keys can either lock or unlock things. Sounds like binding and loosing, doesn't it? Remember, a key does all the work. Even though you are using the key, you're still not the one unlocking or locking anything. The key is doing it. One of the most important keys we've been given, is the Name of Jesus. Let the Name to all the work. Since the devil and his demons are forbidden from operating in Heaven, we can forbid them from operating in our lives on the earth.

Don't forget Matthew 6:9,10. The Lord told us to pray for God's will in Heaven to be done on the earth. There's no poverty, lack, sin, disease or curse in Heaven. Those things are bound out of Heaven. As resurrected men and women in Christ, we have a right to bind all the works of the devil out of our lives! Anything the devil brings against us, we can forbid it from operating in our lives, and it will have to go (Luke 10:19)! When you command the works of darkness to leave you in Jesus' Name; expect it to happen! Health, life, joy, peace and prosperity are loosed in Heaven, they are permitted to operate freely there; so expect the same thing down here. Expect the blessings of Heaven to be manifested in your life right now! Whatever is permitted in Heaven, you can expect to be permitted in your life on this earth, and don't let the devil talk you out of it! When you command your body to be healed, prosperity to come to you, your mind to be at peace, the devil to take his hands off your family, marriage, ministry and job; expect it to happen. You have the keys! You were made alive and resurrected with Christ! You passed through the heavens and Hell couldn't stop you, and sat down at the Father's right hand, in Christ! God has done everything for you and me! Let's start walking, living and ministering as resurrected men and women! We truly are triumphant in Him!!

About the Author

Dwayne Norman is a 1978 graduate of Christ For The Nations Bible Institute in Dallas, Texas. He spent 3 years witnessing to prostitutes and pimps in the red light district of Dallas, and another 3 years ministering as a team leader in the Campus Challenge ministry of Dr. Norvel Hayes. He was ordained by Pastor Buddy and Pat Harrison of Faith Christian Fellowship in Tulsa, Oklahoma in September 1980, and is part of Dr. Ed Dufresne's Fresh Oil Fellowship. He also taught evangelism classes several times at Dr. Hayes' Bible school in Tennessee.

Soon the Lord led him to go on the road ministering. He ministers powerfully on soul winning, and on how God wants to use all Believers in demonstrating His Kingdom not just in Word but also in Power!

He teaches with clarity, the work that God accomplished for all believers in Christ from the cross to the throne, and the importance of this revelation to the church for the fulfillment of Jesus' commission to make disciples of all nations.

He strongly believes that we are called to do the works Jesus did and greater works in His Name, not just in church but especially in the market place. As a result Dwayne experiences many healing miracles in his services, arms and legs growing out, as well as other miracles.

He and his wife Leia travel and teach Supernatural Evangelism and train Believers in who they are in Christ and how to operate in their ministries.

To inquire for meetings with Dwayne & Leia Norman, please contact them at:

Dwayne & Leia Norman
124 Evergreen Court
Mt. Sterling, KY   40353

(859) 351-6496
dwayne7@att.net
Web: www.dwaynenormanministries.org

Contact Dwayne to order his other books and products:

The Mystery DVD's (12 hours)	$50.00
The Mystery (book)	$12.00
The Mystery Study Guide	$10.00
The Awesome Power in the Message of the Cross	$10.00
Your Beginning with God	$10.00
The Law of the Spirit of Life in Christ Jesus	$10.00
Demonstrating God's Kingdom	$10.00